Androcles and the Lion

Retold by Jenny Giles
Illustrated by Loma Tilders

NELSON PRICE MILBURN

Long, long ago, a wealthy landowner lived near the city of Rome. He had many slaves, and one of them was a man called Androcles.

Androcles and some of the other slaves had to work hard in the fields all day long. Their master was very cruel, and they were given little to eat or drink. If they stopped to rest, for even a short time, they were shouted at, and lashed with whips.

Although Androcles had been treated roughly all his life, he was still a gentle man. He took good care of his master's horses, and was always kind to the mice and rabbits and birds who lived in the fields.

Animals trusted him.

After some years, Androcles' master sailed to Africa, taking many of his slaves with him. Androcles was among them and, when he arrived in Africa, he was made to work even harder than before. He was always hot and tired and hungry.

One day, when his master had been even more cruel than usual, Androcles decided that he would leave, and never return. He knew that his life would be in danger if he were caught, so he planned his escape carefully.

He waited until there was a dark, cloudy night with no moon or stars. Then he crept away, and fled down the empty road.

Androcles kept running all through the night and, when morning came, he found himself in a barren land. The day was going to be very hot; the sun was already rising in the clear blue sky.

By this time, Androcles was very tired, so he looked around for somewhere to hide and rest. In the distance he could see some hills, so he stumbled towards them as the sun blazed down on him.

Androcles was exhausted when he reached the hills. He found a cave in the rocks, and crawled into it. It was cool and dark inside the cave, and very peaceful.

"My master will never be able to find me here," he said to himself. He lay down and immediately fell into a deep sleep.

Suddenly Androcles was woken by a loud roar. He leaped to his feet and, to his horror, saw a great lion. Its mouth was open, and Androcles could see its sharp teeth as it roared again.

Androcles was terrified! The lion was blocking the entrance to the cave, and there was no way he could escape. Shaking with fear, he waited for it to spring upon him.

But the lion did not move, except to lift its front paw. As Androcles watched, the lion licked its paw and then roared once more, as if in pain. Androcles could see that a long, sharp thorn had gone deep into the paw.

Forgetting his fear, Androcles knelt down beside the lion, as he had done so often before with smaller animals. Somehow, the lion seemed to know that it could trust him.

Androcles gripped the thorn and pulled swiftly. As the thorn came out, the lion growled in pain. But instead of harming Androcles, it lay down beside him and began to lick the swollen paw.

From that moment on, Androcles and the lion became friends. Androcles found shelter in the cave, and the lion led him to a small oasis where there was water to drink and food to eat.

And so Androcles lived happily with the lion for many weeks.

But one day, Androcles was careless. He went walking far away from the cave, and was seen by some soldiers, who were out looking for runaway slaves.

The soldiers laughed among themselves as they captured Androcles. "We will take this slave back to his master and we will get a good reward for him," they said.

Androcles' cruel master was delighted that his slave had been recaptured. But he was furious with Androcles, and sent him back to Rome to be punished. There he was thrown into a cramped prison cell, and made to wait until there was a special holiday.

On special holidays in Rome, everyone came to watch prisoners being forced to fight against wild animals. Thousands of people came to see these contests in the arena. For them, it was thrilling entertainment. They did not care that slaves were hurt or killed: they shouted and cheered as the fights went on.

When the emperor arrived, the contests began.

Soon it was Androcles' turn. He heard the noise of the crowd as the soldiers dragged him out into the arena. He was given a small spear to use, and then left standing all alone. He looked up at the rows of people seated high above him. They were all waiting in excitement for his fight to start.

Androcles knew what would happen next. A starving wild animal would be brought into the arena, and he would have to fight it, or die. He watched in terror as a huge lion was brought up into the arena in a cage.

As soon as the cage door was opened, the lion gave a loud roar and sprang towards Androcles.

But at that moment, Androcles knew that he could not harm any animal, no matter how fierce it was, and no matter how frightened he was. He dropped the spear, and stood quite still, waiting for the lion's sharp claws and teeth to strike him.

Then, suddenly, the lion stopped charging!

It gazed at Androcles, and padded across the arena towards him.

Then the great, fierce lion stood in front of Androcles. Slowly, it lowered its head and licked Androcles' hand. The crowd fell silent and watched in amazement.

Androcles sighed with relief as he recognised his old friend from the cave! He put one arm around the lion's mane, and man and beast stood side by side.

There would be no fight between Androcles and this lion...

Instead of being angry, everyone in the crowd cheered! Never before had they seen such a sight!

The emperor was astonished by the power that Androcles seemed to have over the lion. Right then and there, he made Androcles a free man, and gave him a purse full of gold.

Now that he was no longer a slave, Androcles could live without fear.

And for many years, people would watch him walking through the streets of Rome, with his friend, the great lion, beside him.

A play
Androcles and the Lion

People in the play

 Reader

 Lion

 Androcles

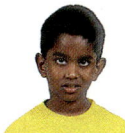 Androcles' master

 Slave

 Emperor

 Two guards

 Two soldiers

 Crowd

Scene One — *A farm near Rome*

Reader

Long ago, a wealthy landowner lived near the city of Rome. He had many slaves, and one of them was a man called Androcles.

Androcles

I am tired of working in the fields with the other slaves day after day. Our master is always cruel to us. He gives us little to eat, and if we stop to have a rest, he whips us.

Reader

Although Androcles had been treated roughly all his life, he was still a gentle man. He took good care of his master's horses, and was always kind to the mice and rabbits and birds who lived in the fields. Animals trusted him.

Slave

I am very tired, but if I stop to have a rest, our master will punish me.

Androcles

There must be some way we can escape.

Slave

I am too afraid to leave. If we were caught, we would be made to fight wild animals in the arena in Rome.

Androcles

You are right. But one day, I will escape.

Reader

Later that year, Androcles' master sailed to Africa, taking many of his slaves with him. Androcles was among them and, when he arrived in Africa, he was made to work even harder than before.

Scene Two — *A farm in Africa*

Androcles

Our master is getting more and more cruel, and I will not stay here and work for him any longer. But I know that if I am caught, my life will be in danger. I must plan my escape very carefully.

Reader

Androcles waited until there was a dark, cloudy night with no moon or stars. Then he crept away, and fled down the empty road.

Androcles

At last I have escaped! I will keep running until I am far away from this place.

Reader

Androcles ran all through the night and, when morning came, he found himself in a barren land. The day was going to be very hot.

Androcles

I have come a long way, and I am very tired. I must find somewhere to hide and rest. I will keep going until I reach those hills.

Reader

Androcles stumbled onwards as the sun blazed down on him. He was exhausted when he reached the hills. He found a cave in the rocks, and crawled into it.

Androcles

It is cool and dark inside this cave. My master will never be able to find me here. At last I can go to sleep without fear.

Reader

Suddenly, Androcles was woken by a loud roar.

Lion   *ROAR!*

Androcles (leaping up)

I must be dreaming! There's a lion standing in the entrance to the cave! I am trapped!

Lion   *ROAR!*

Reader

Shaking with fear, Androcles waited for the lion to spring upon him. But the lion did not move, except to lift its front paw.

Lion (licking its paw)   *Roar!*

Androcles (to the lion)

I can see a long, sharp thorn in your paw!

Reader

Forgetting his fear, Androcles knelt down beside the lion. Somehow, the lion seemed to know that it could trust him.

Androcles

I can pull this thorn out of your paw.

Reader

Androcles pulled the thorn out swiftly.

Lion (licking its paw)   *Grr! Grr!*

Androcles

You were roaring because you were in pain! You are not going to harm me.

Reader

From that moment on, Androcles and the lion became friends. Androcles found shelter in the cave, and the lion led him to a small oasis where there was water to drink, and food to eat. And so Androcles lived with the lion for many weeks. Then one day, Androcles decided to go for a walk.

Androcles

I am tired of staying in this cave. I am going for a long walk today.

Reader

But Androcles was careless. He went far away from the cave, and was captured by soldiers, who were looking for runaway slaves.

First soldier (laughing)

We will take this slave back to his master.

Second soldier

And we will get a good reward for him!

Reader

The soldiers took Androcles back to his master.

Master

You have done well! Here is your reward. As for you, Androcles, I am sending you back to Rome to be punished.

Scene Three — In Rome

Reader

On special days in Rome, everyone came to watch the prisoners who were forced to fight against wild animals.

Androcles

The day for my punishment has arrived. All the other slaves have been taken into the arena. Soon it will be my turn to die.

First guard

You must come with us now.

Second guard

You are going to have to fight a lion, and you can use only this small spear. Here! Take it!

Reader

Androcles looked up at the rows of people seated high above him. They were all waiting for his fight to start. He watched in terror as a lion was brought into the arena. As soon as the cage door was opened, the lion gave a loud roar and sprang towards Androcles.

Lion   *ROAR!*

Androcles

I will not fight this lion! I cannot harm any animal, no matter how fierce it is.

Reader

So Androcles dropped the spear and stood quite still, waiting for the lion's sharp claws and teeth to strike him.

Androcles

Nothing can save me now!

Reader

Suddenly, the lion stopped charging! It gazed at Androcles, and padded across the arena towards him. Then, slowly, it lowered its head and licked his hand. The crowd watched in amazement, and fell silent.

Androcles (standing beside the lion)

This lion is my old friend from the cave! There will be no fight between the two of us.

Reader

Instead of being angry, the crowd cheered. Never before had they seen such a sight!

Crowd (clapping and cheering)

Hurrah! Hurrah! Let the slave live!

Emperor (calling Androcles)

I am astonished by the power that you have over this lion. I am going to make you a free man, and give you a purse of gold.

Androcles

This lion is my friend. He will not harm anyone while he is with me. Please let him go free as well.

Emperor

This magnificent animal can indeed go free.

Androcles

Now that I am no longer a slave, I can live without fear. And I will always take care of my good friend, the lion.

Reader

And, for many years, people would watch Androcles walking through the streets of Rome with his friend, the great lion, beside him.